POWER YOUR CREATIVE BRAIN 3

Jan Parker

ideas

OUR WORLD

write

draw

dreams

enjoy

songs

Colour & Create

ART THERAPY - BASED EXERCISES

For Sian

First published March 2018

PARKER PUBLICATIONS

ART WORK Jan Parker

TECHNICAL EDITOR Matthew Fordham

ISBN 978-0-9957498-4-9

4

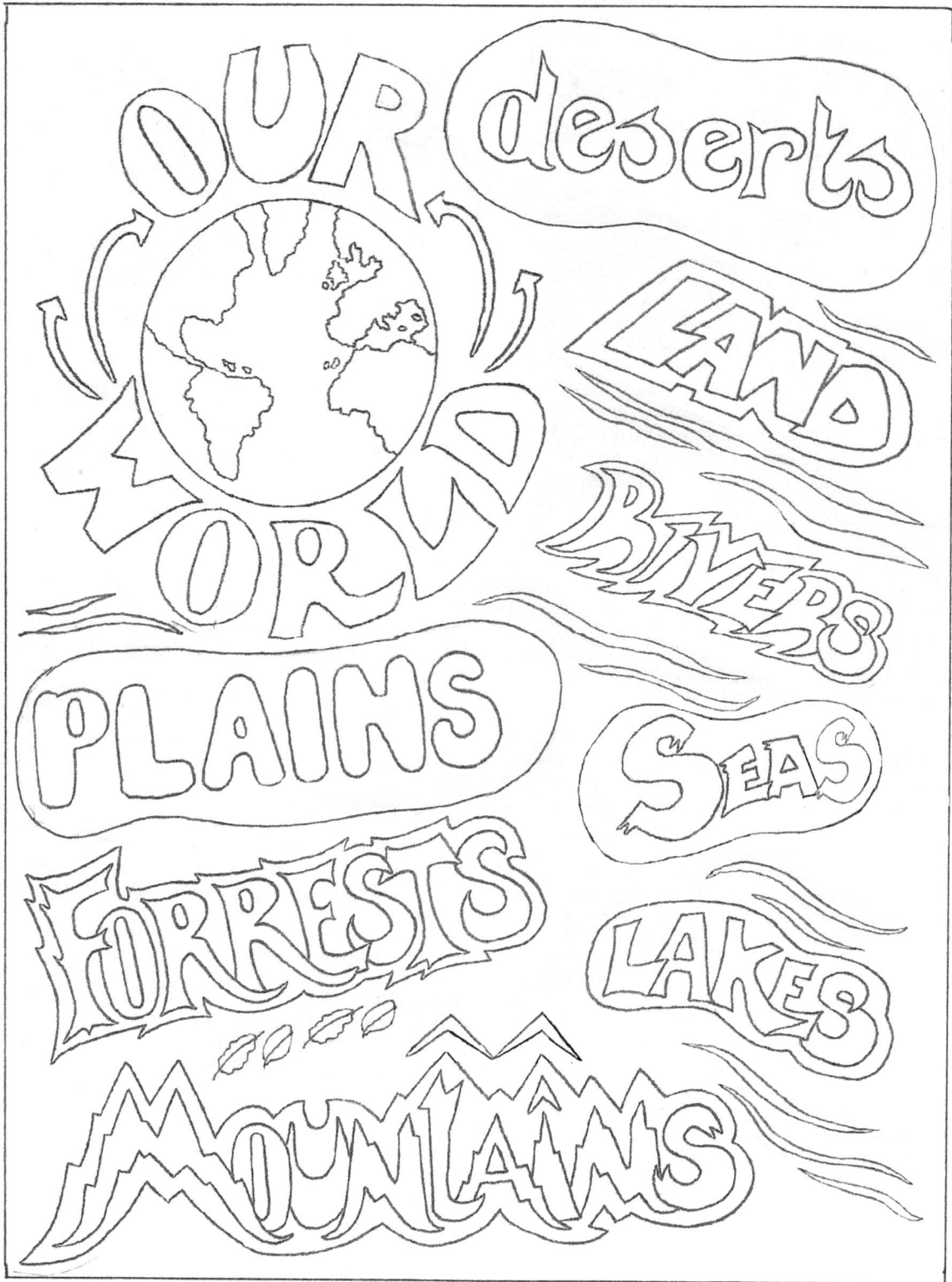

OUR deserts WORLD LAND RIVERS PLAINS SEAS FORRESTS LAKES MOUNTAINS

Your thoughts + notes

Your drawings + ideas

songs

OUR WORLD

Memories

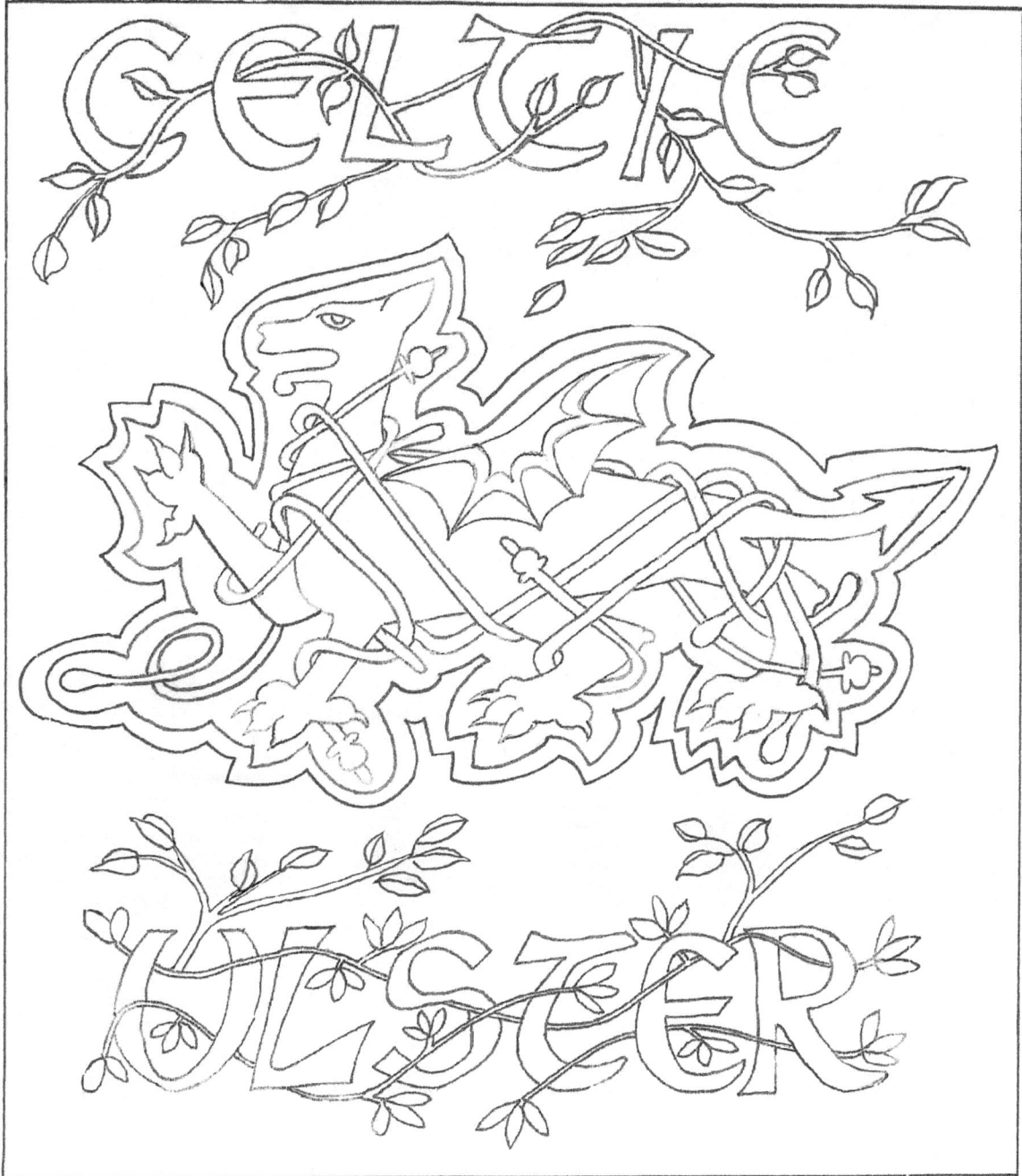

CELTIC

drawings + ideas

Fashion

Book cover

songs

Your thoughts + notes

POWER YOUR CREATIVE BRAIN

OUR BIRDS

Swan

Skylark

Ducks

Wren

Dove

Robin

Eagle

Heron

Blackbird

Your thoughts + notes

Your drawings + ideas

pets

dreams

memories

BiRDS

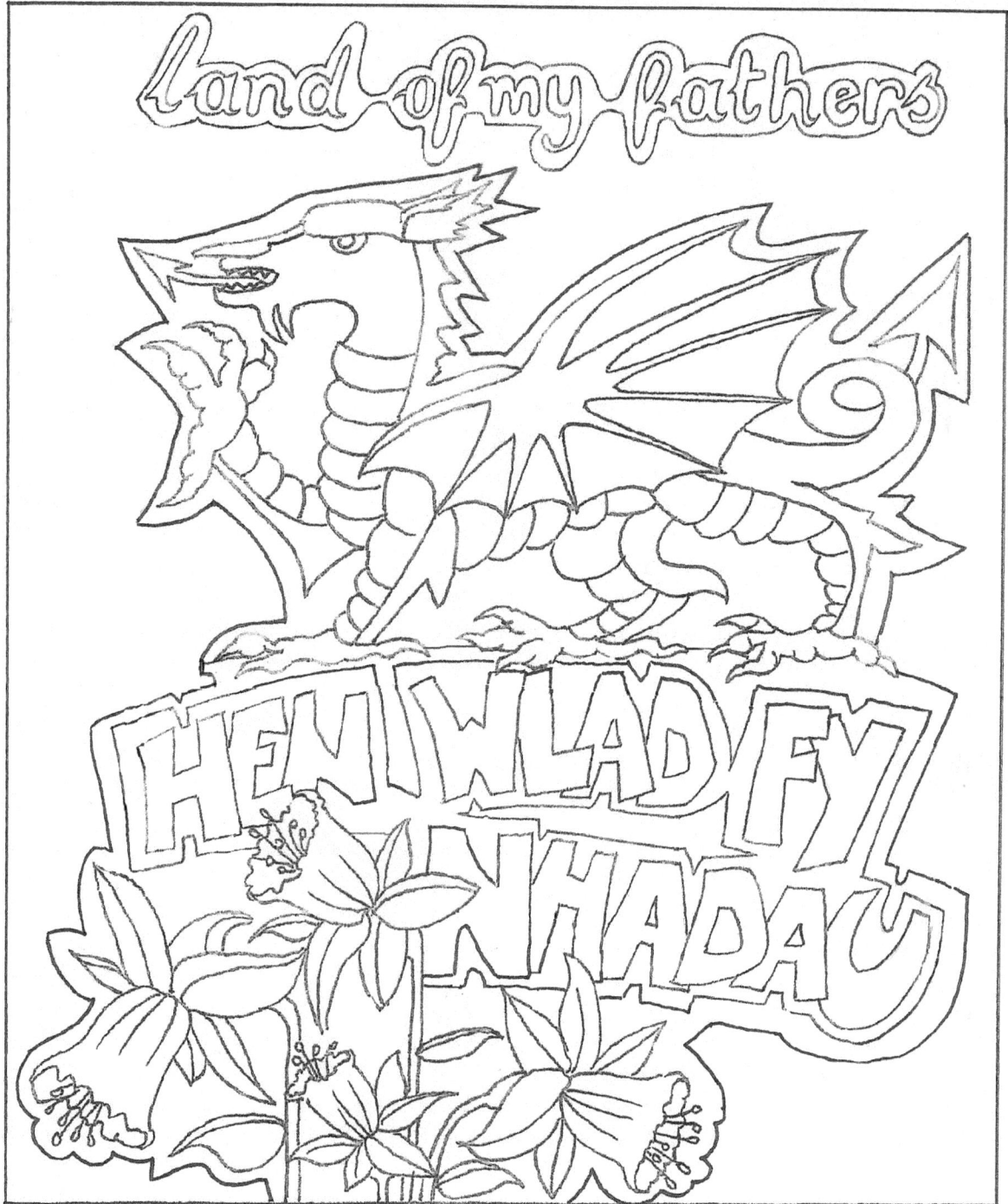

Handout

memories

LAND OF MY FATHERS

Your drawings + ideas

Your poems + songs

Book cover

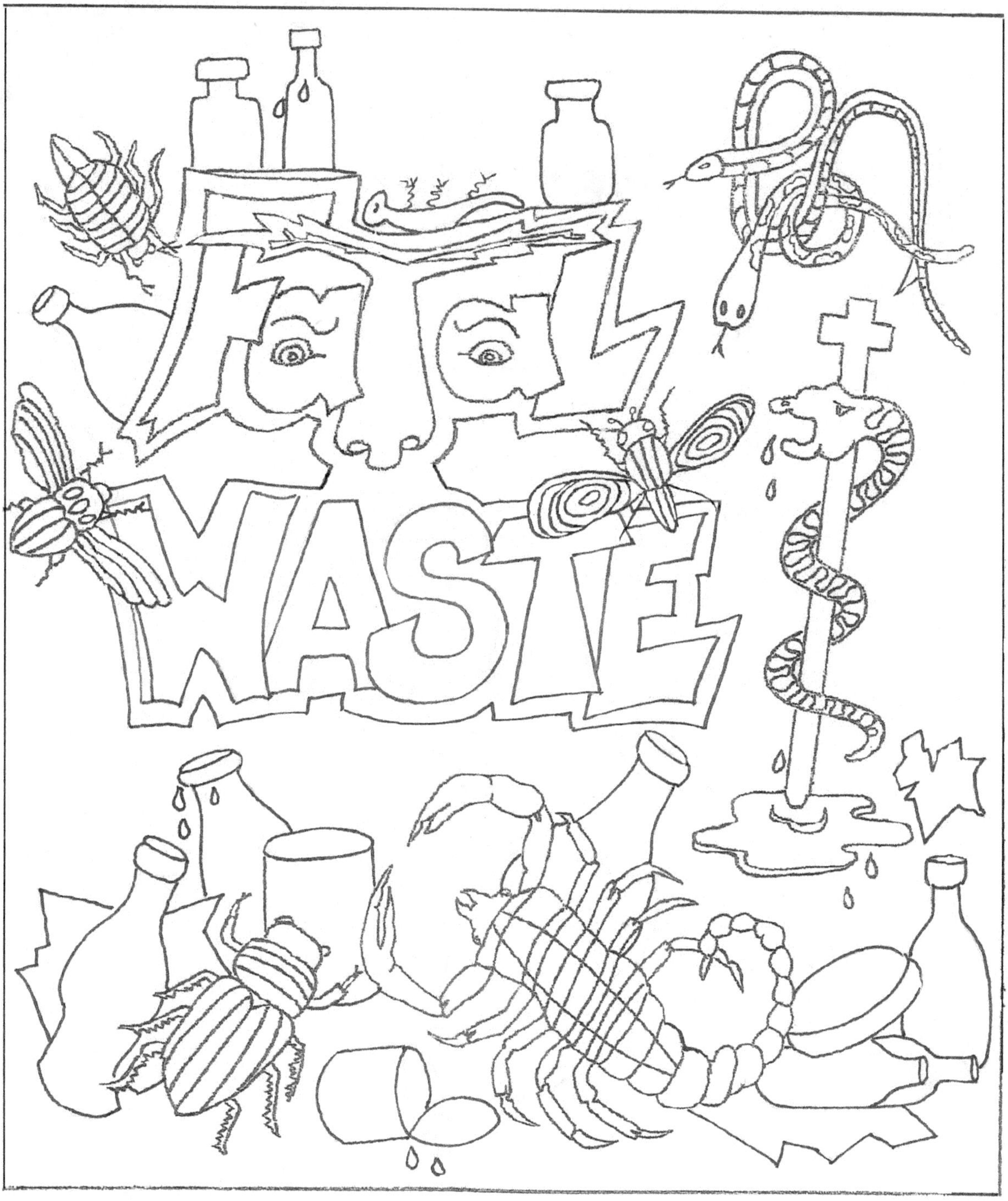
Fatal
WASTE

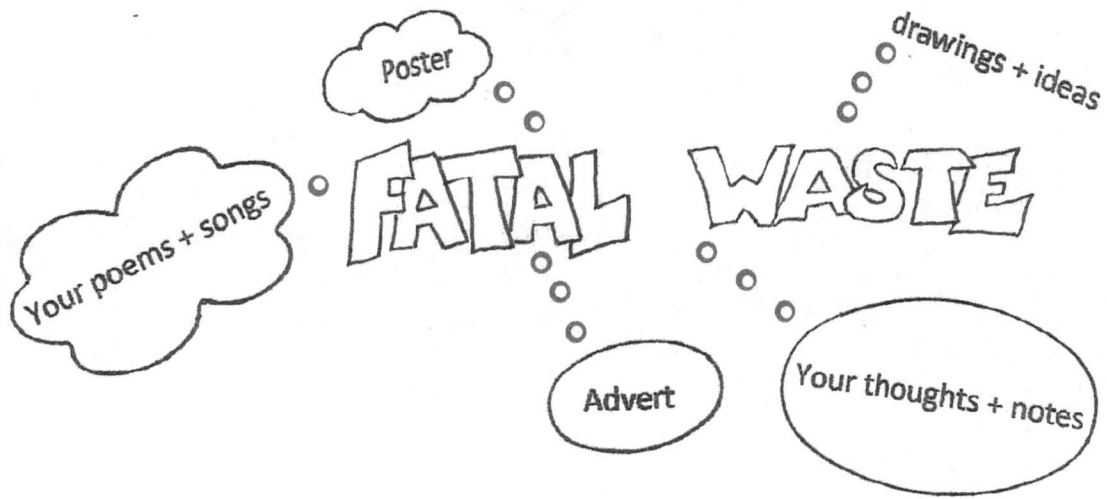

Your poems + songs

Poster

FATAL WASTE

drawings + ideas

Advert

Your thoughts + notes

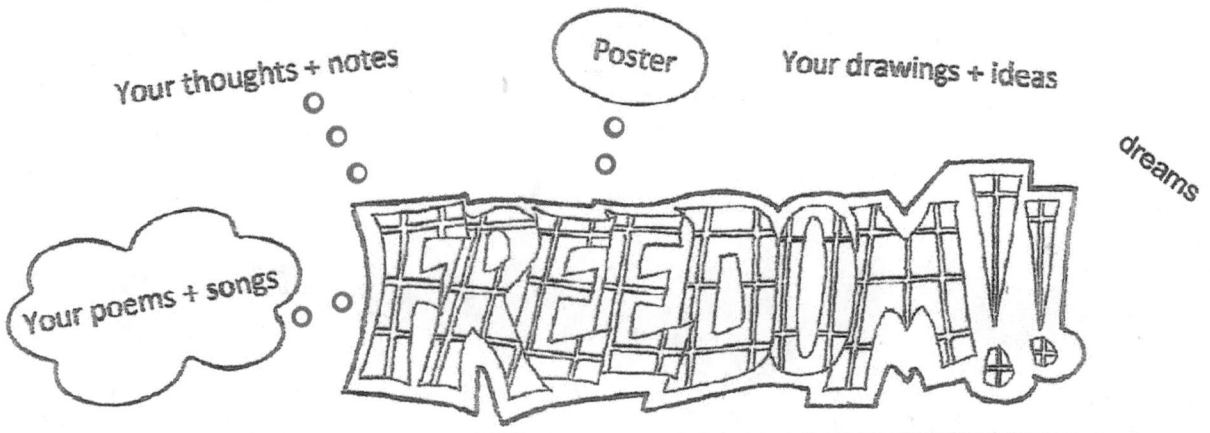

Your thoughts + notes

Poster

Your drawings + ideas

dreams

Your poems + songs

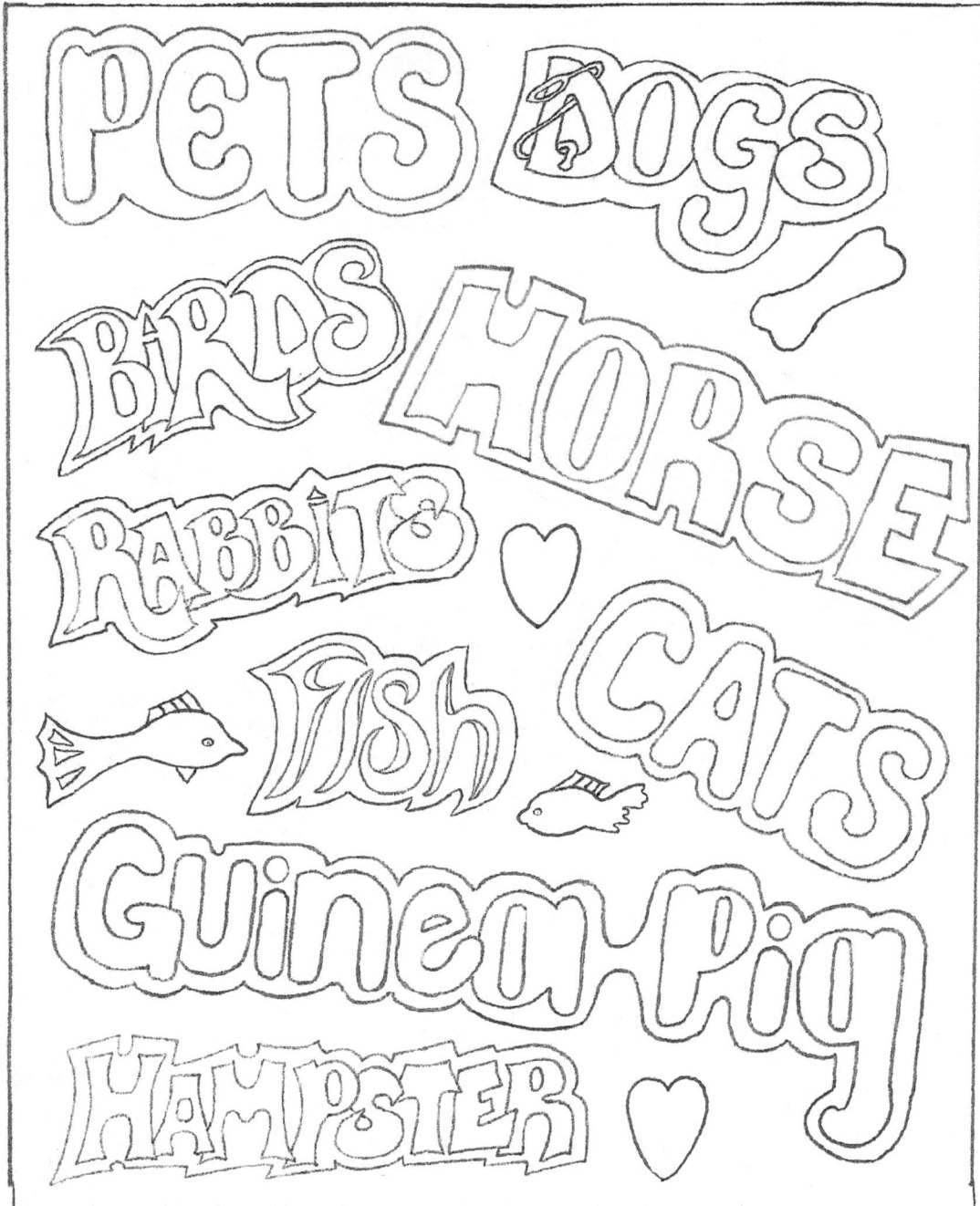

PETS DOGS
BIRDS HORSE
RABBITS
FISH CATS
Guinea Pig
HAMPSTER

memories

PETS

Your drawings + ideas

Your poems + songs

Handout

Book cover

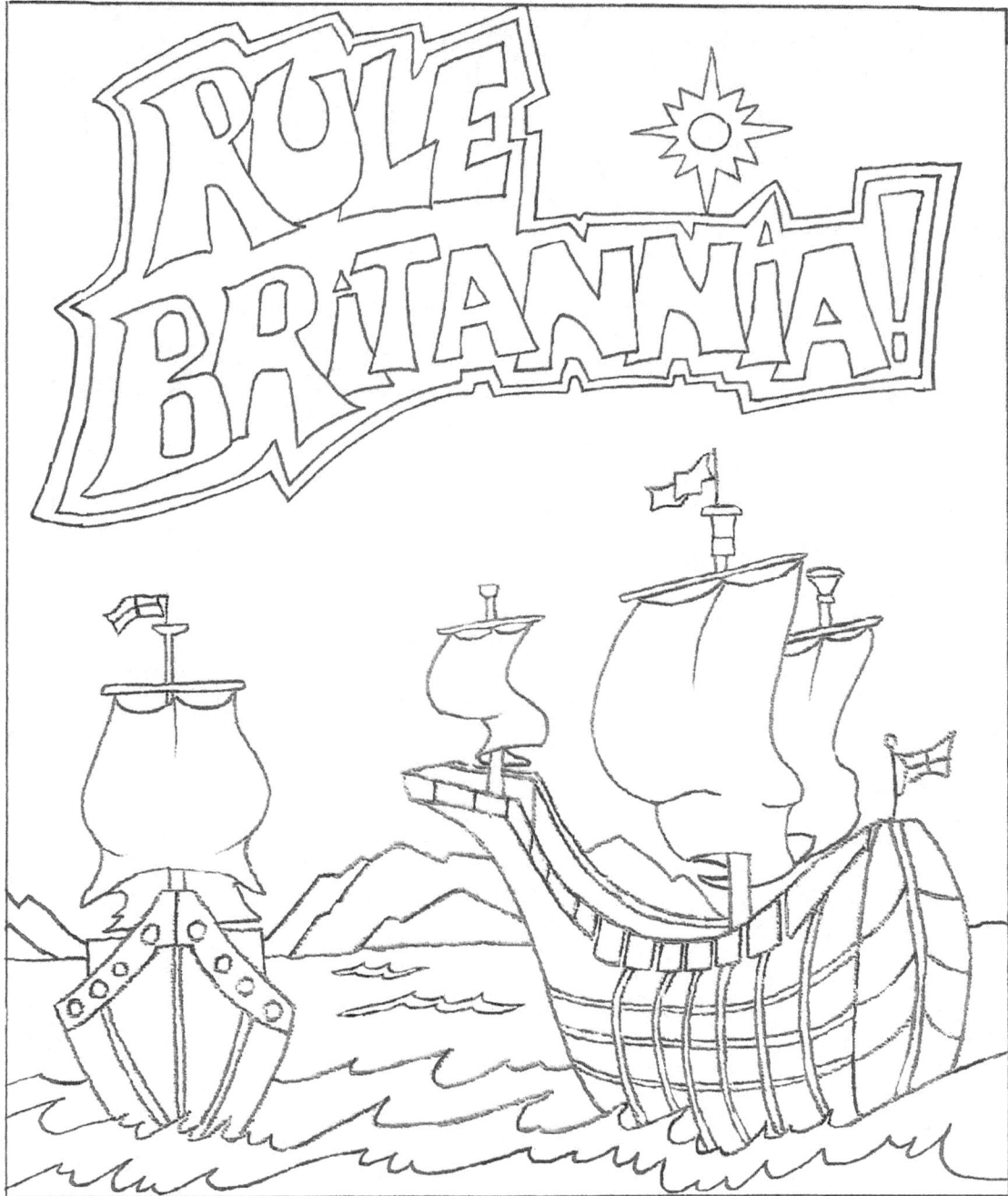

RULE BRITANNIA

drawings + ideas

Poster

Book cover

dreams

Your poems + songs

Your thoughts + notes

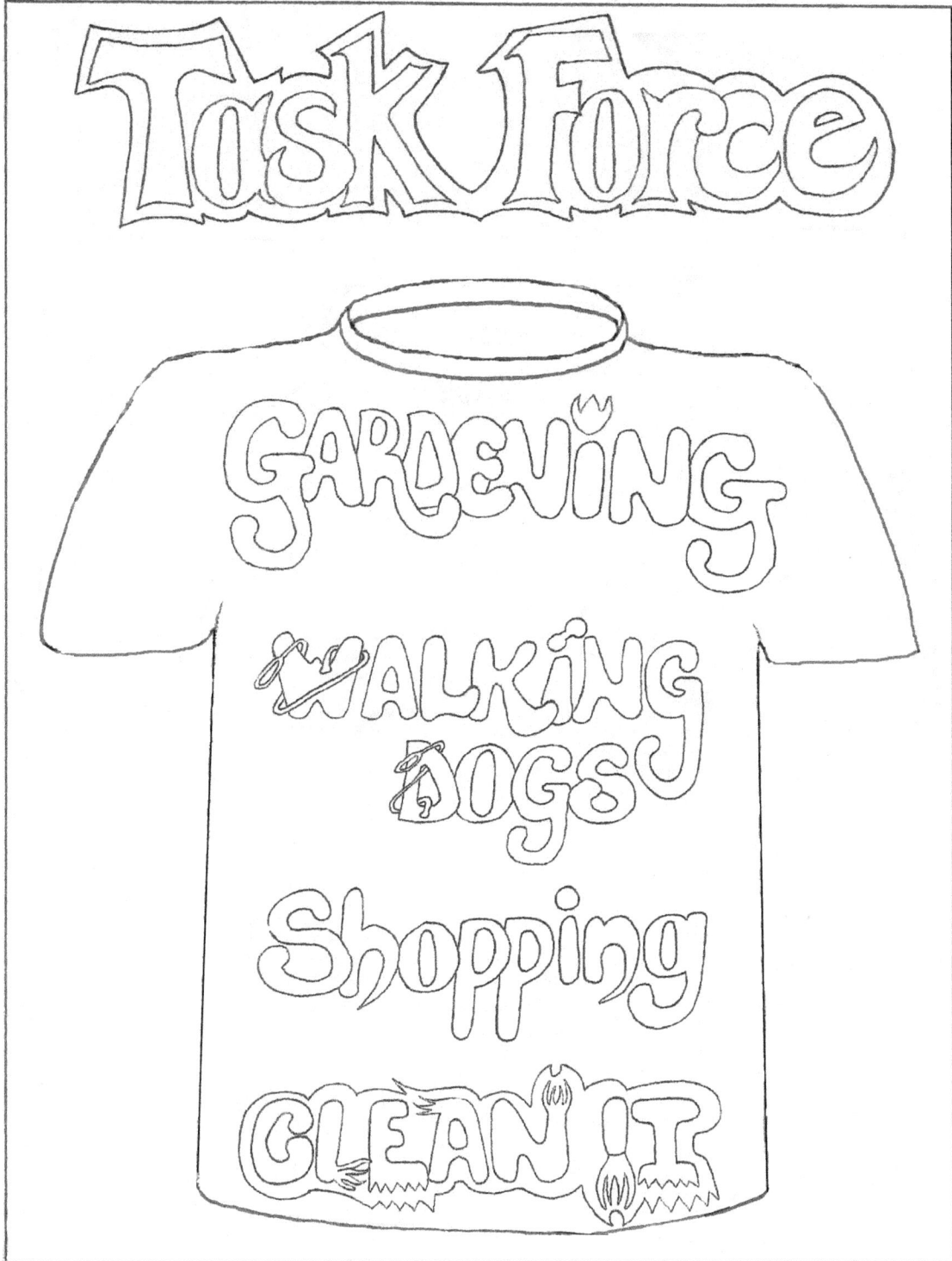

Task Force

GARDENING

WALKING DOGS

Shopping

CLEAN IT

Task Force

Poster

Handout

thoughts + notes

Your drawings + ideas

Your drawings + ideas

thoughts + notes

Your poems + songs

Advert

Poster

Fashion

WILD LIFE

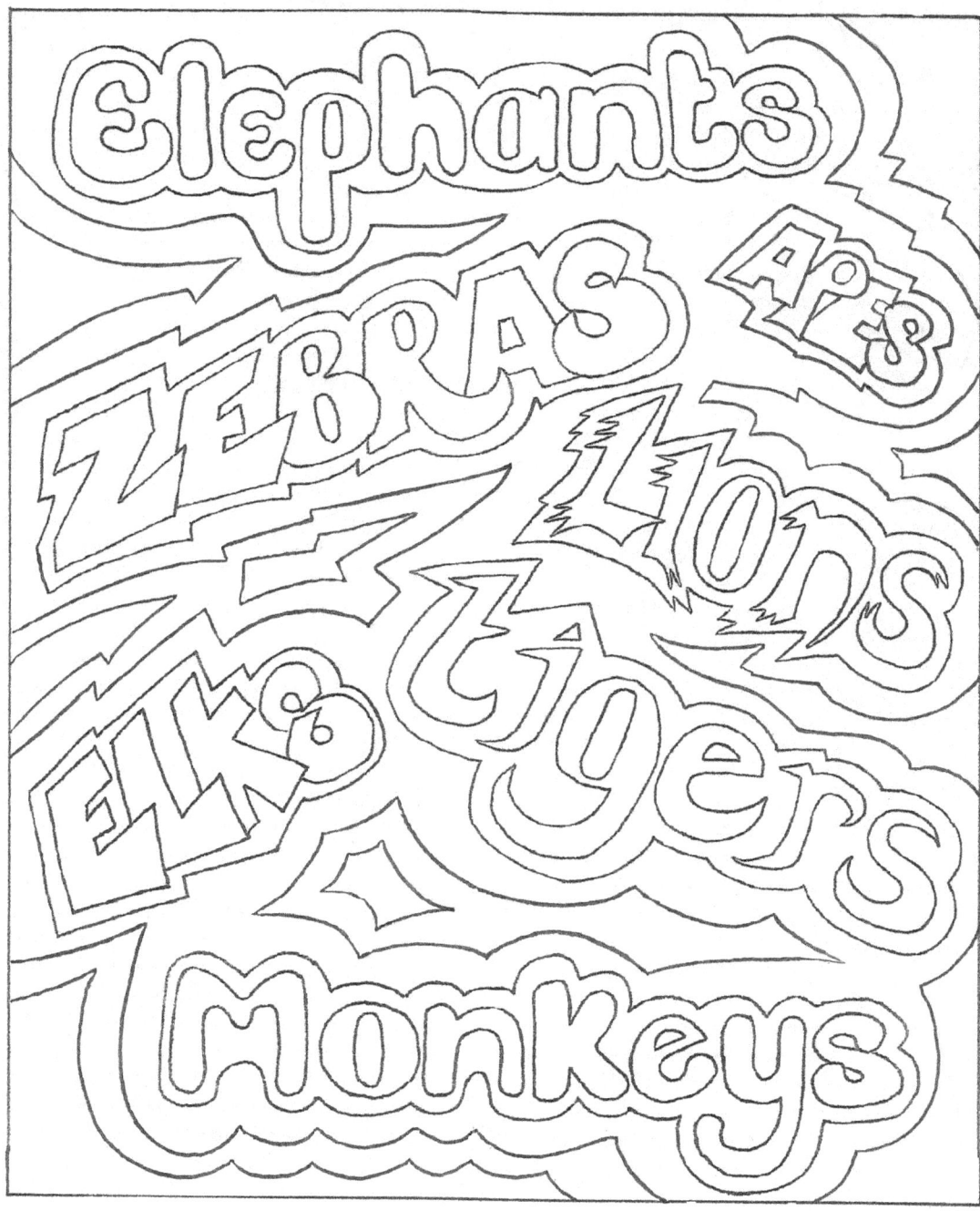

WILD LIFE

drawings + ideas

Book cover

Poster

Your thoughts + notes

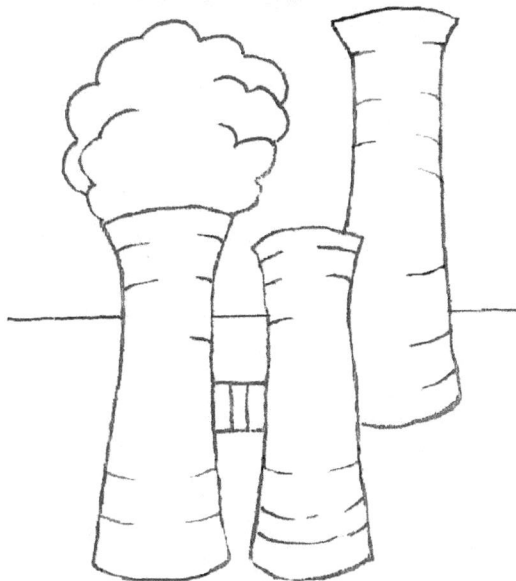

Your drawings + ideas

Handout

PROTEST

Your thoughts + notes

Book cover

Poster

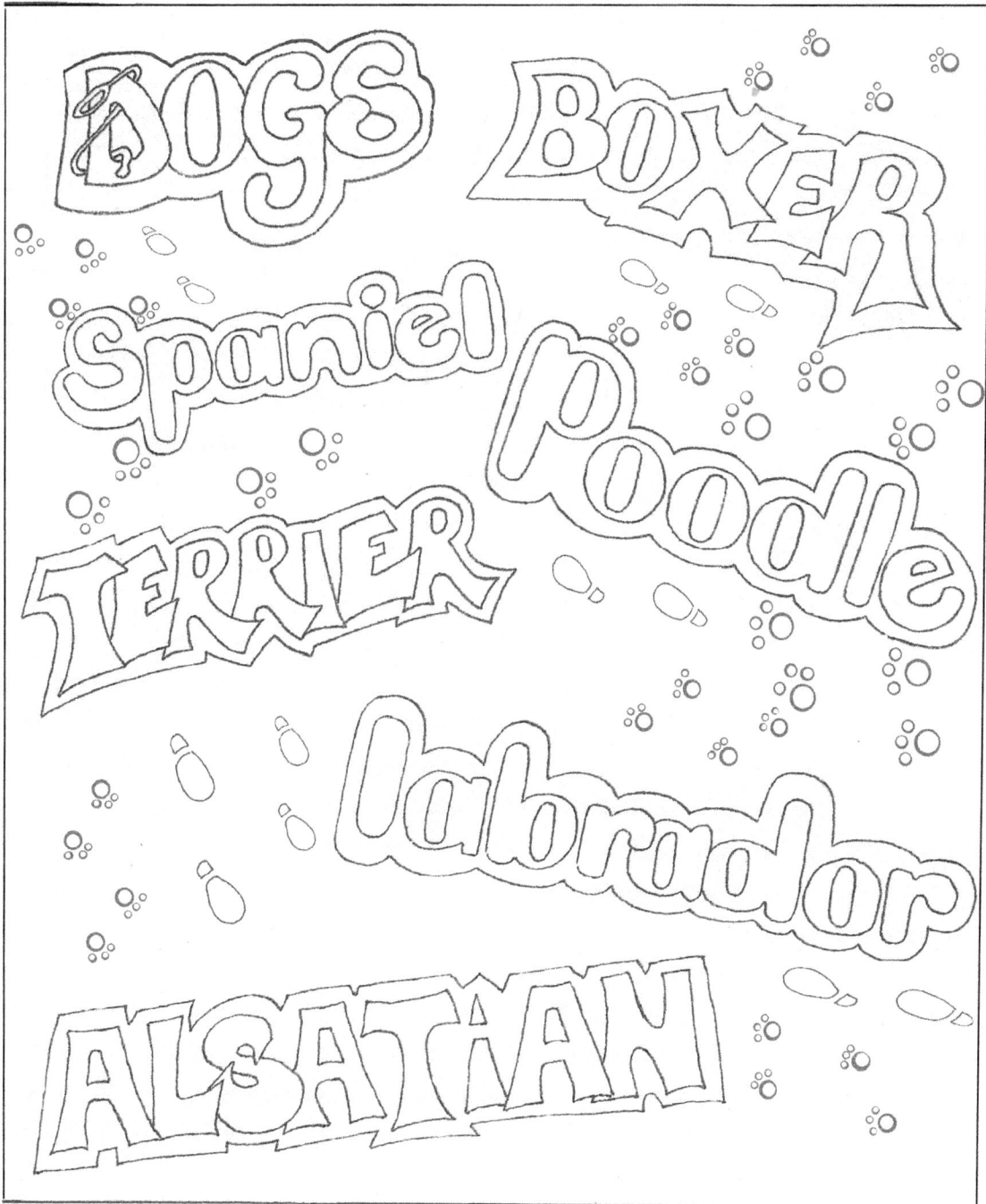

Your drawings + ideas

Your thoughts + notes

pets

Advert

DOGS

hobbies

Your drawings + ideas

Poster

Handout

thoughts + notes

SAVE-US

Advert

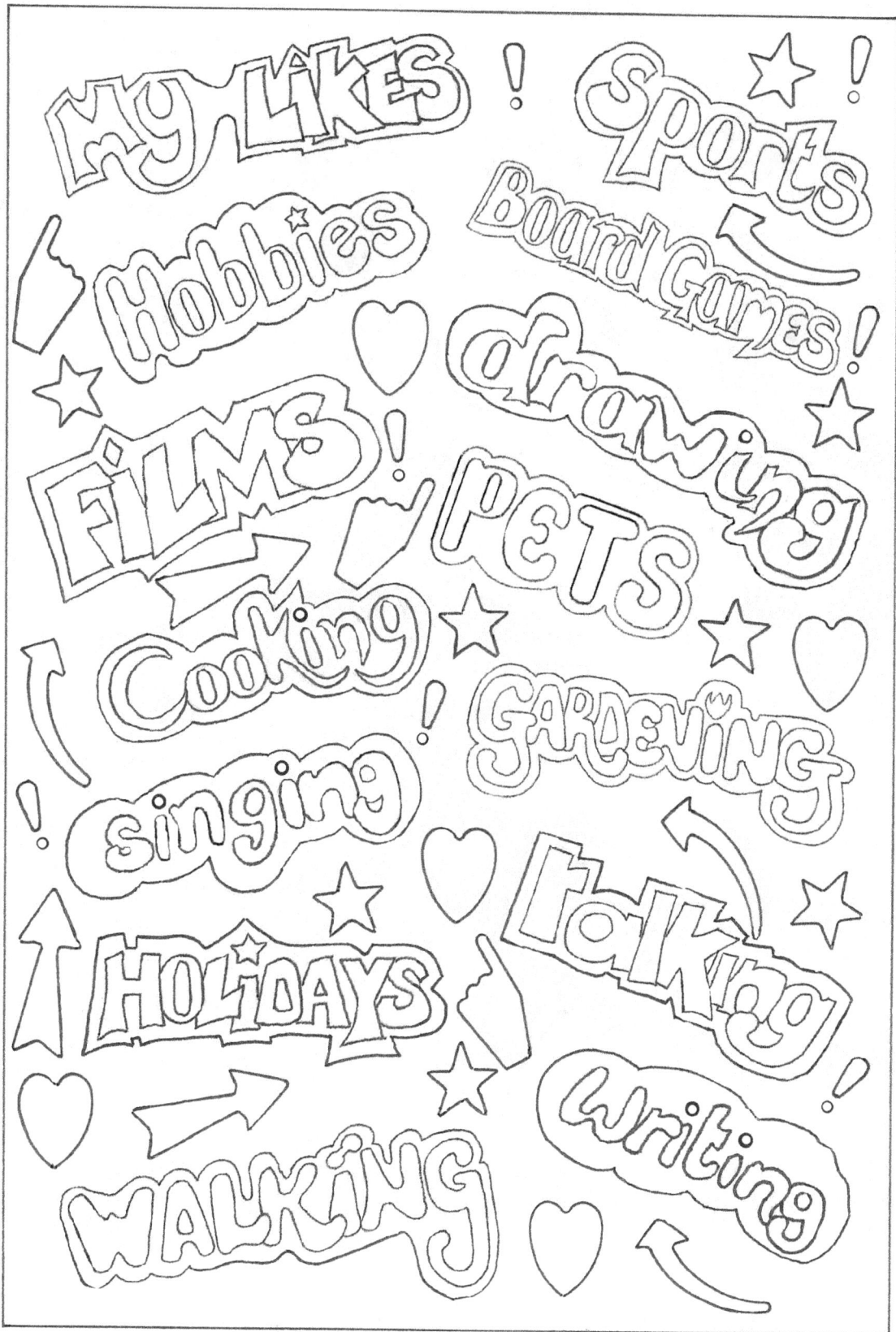

My LIKES !   Sports ☆ !

Hobbies   Board Games !

Films !   drawing

Cooking   PETS

singing !   Gardening

Holidays   talking !

Walking   Writing

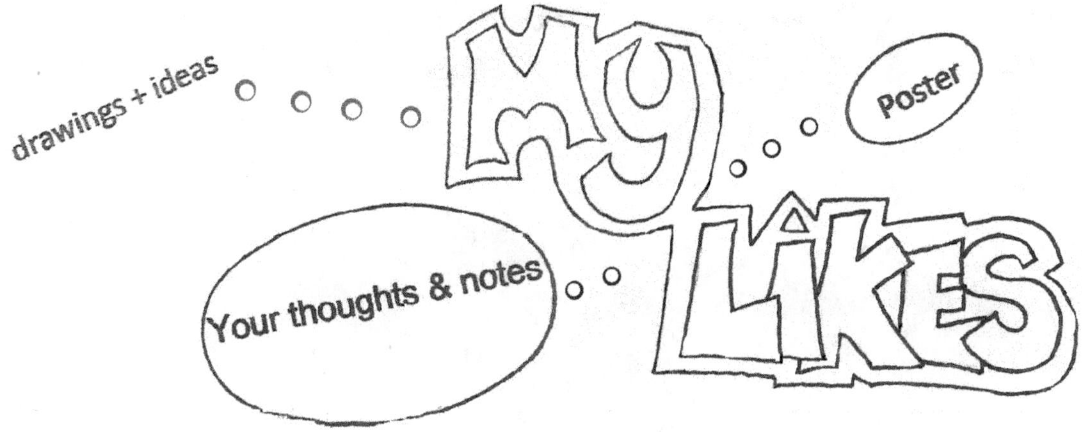
drawings + ideas
My
Poster
Your thoughts & notes
Likes

Poster

drawings + ideas

DON'T BULLY ME

Your thoughts & notes

feelings

Advert

Handout

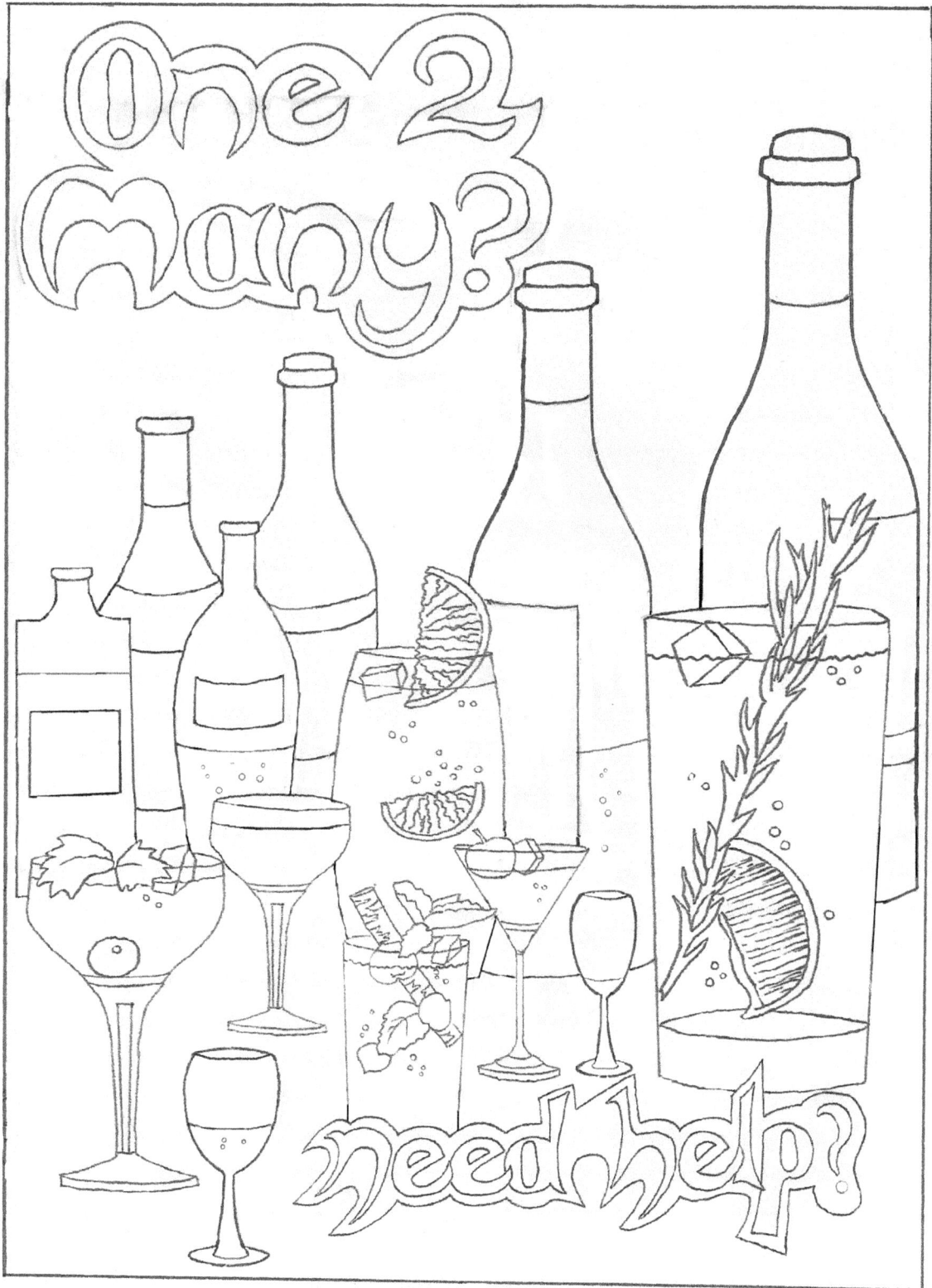

drawings + ideas

Poster

Your thoughts & notes

One 2 Many?

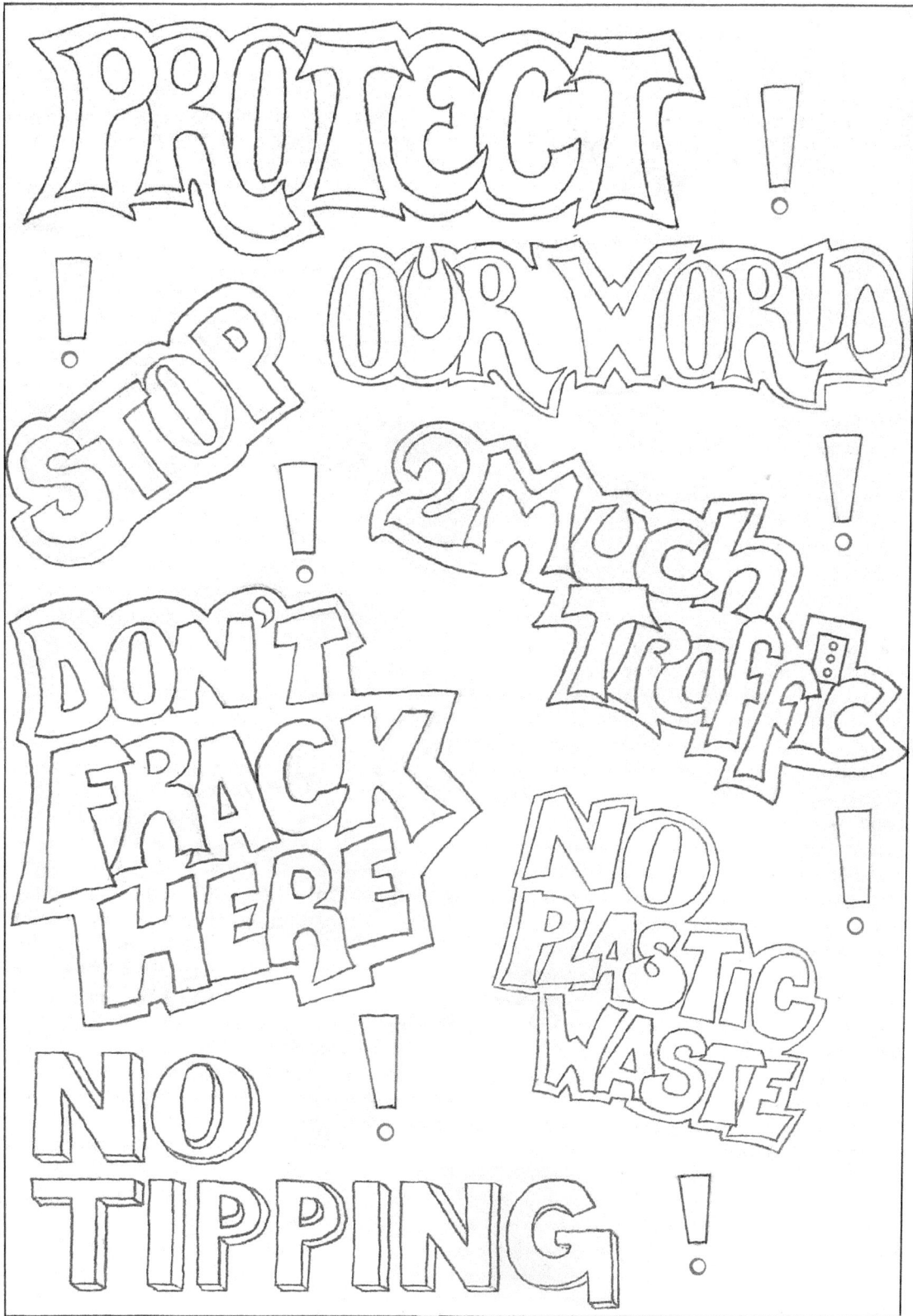

PROTECT OUR WORLD

Your drawings + ideas

Poster

Book cover

Your thoughts + notes